Introduction

Motorbikes have been a favourite form of transport for over 100 years. Many famous historical figures rode motorbikes. Lawrence of Arabia, for instance, had a Brough Superior and the first man to cross the Atlantic Ocean by plane, Charles Lindbergh, rode a Harley-Davidson. Today, motorbike riding is just as popular, but the variety of bikes you can buy has increased enormously.

This picture gives you a first look at the parts which make up a modern motorbike. The bike is a 1,000 cc BMW K1, with the fairing cut away to reveal the engine.

In this book you will fi
motorbikes, from a stu.
sports roadster to a nippy little 125 cc trail bike. Tyres, brakes, engines - they are all explained clearly, together with tips on choosing your first bike. There is even a section that starts you off on the road to becoming a safe and competent rider.

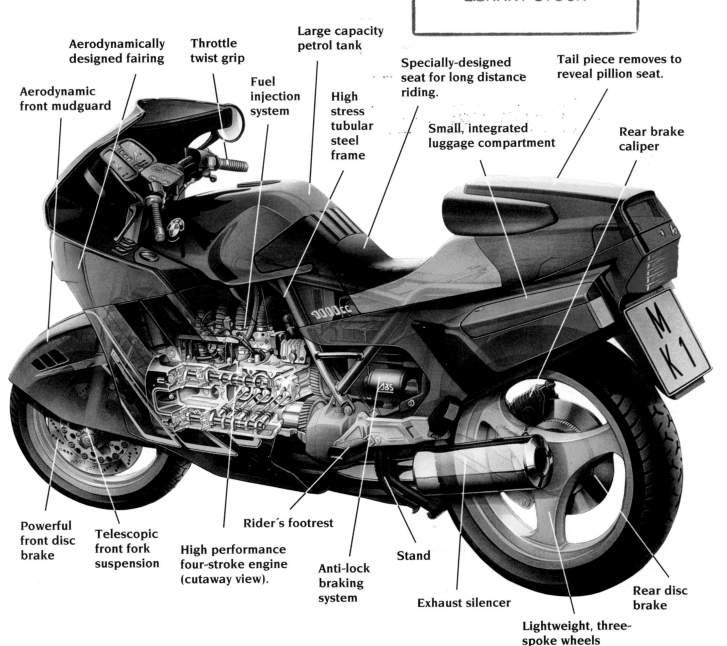

Aerodynamically designed fairing

Aerodynamic front mudguard

Throttle twist grip

Fuel injection system

Large capacity petrol tank

High stress tubular steel frame

Specially-designed seat for long distance riding.

Small, integrated luggage compartment

Tail piece removes to reveal pillion seat.

Rear brake caliper

Powerful front disc brake

Telescopic front fork suspension

High performance four-stroke engine (cutaway view).

Rider's footrest

Anti-lock braking system

Stand

Exhaust silencer

Lightweight, three-spoke wheels

Rear disc brake

Motorbike testing

Motorbikes start life as experimental prototypes which are ridden mercilessly over special test tracks. They are also tested on long distance runs in all types of weather and traffic conditions. The aim is to discover any weak points and correct a bike's design accordingly. Next the assembly lines for mass production are prepared. The first bikes off the assembly line are called pre-production models and these too are thoroughly tested. When the manufacturers are finally satisfied with the design, actual production begins. Motorbike magazines publish road test reports on new bikes to help prospective customers. This test, on a fast roadster, was written specially for this book.

Kawasaki GPZ900R road test

The Kawasaki GPZ900R is a fast bike - and looks it. The full fairing was designed in a wind tunnel and gives the bike its sleek lines. Many of the bike's features have originated from the Kawasaki Grand Prix racing bikes.

Sitting in the saddle, you can immediately appreciate how compact the bike is, especially the incredibly narrow engine. Four-cylinder, in-line engines are usually quite bulky, but by using liquid cooling and repositioning the generator, overall width has been trimmed considerably. This means the engine can be mounted low in the frame, without reducing cornering clearance.

Starting and stopping

A touch of the starter button and the engine springs into life. Vibration is virtually non-existent, but choke is needed for about 1.6 km (1 mile) as the engine warms up to operating temperature, which is regulated by the radiator.

The front wheel with a radius of 43 cm (17 in) means that steering is light, even in heavy traffic, and gives excellent straight line stability.

Road-holding and braking are superb thanks to the grippy wide section tyres, the dual 300 mm (12 in) semi-floating discs and the anti-dive, air-assisted front fork which stops the front end dipping suddenly under fierce braking.

The Kawasaki GPZ900R sports bike built for high speeds.

The GPZ900R's diamond frame

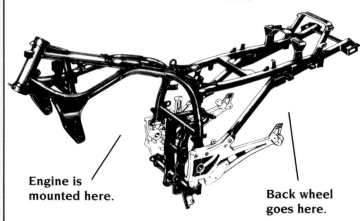

Engine is mounted here.

Back wheel goes here.

The lightweight diamond frame is massively strong and acts as an excellent "backbone" for the bike. An alloy subframe is bolted on to it at the rear. The engine is mounted low down on the frame, giving a low centre of gravity, which means the bike is better balanced and road handling improves. It is possible to mount the engine so low due to the lack of down tubes, and tubes below the crankcase. This has allowed the exhaust pipes to be tucked in, giving room for the engine closer to the ground.

Good handling at speed

The GPZ900R is a sports bike built for high speeds. In 1984, its first year of production, it set new performance standards and finished 1, 2 and 3 in the Isle of Man TT Production Race.

It is on winding, traffic-free roads that the bike really excels. The low-set handlebars provide a comfortable crouched riding position. This is important at high speeds because the more a rider can tuck in behind the fairing, the less he interferes with the fairing's specially-designed aerodynamic shape. Another important reason for such a position is that the fairing can protect a rider in bad weather conditions.

Rear suspension is Kawasaki's championship-winning Uni-Trak system. This employs a single shock absorber with progressive action. Hitting a pothole at high speed will not cause the suspension to bottom out and throw the bike off course. Small irregularities in the road are easily absorbed to give the rider a smooth, comfortable journey.

With all these features and its lightweight chassis, the GPZ900R is a machine that handles exceptionally well. Straight-line stability is perfect, and the light, quick steering means that a series of bends can be taken safely at high speed.

THE USBORNE YOUNG SCIENTIST
MOTORBIKES

Contents

Credits

Written by Philip Chapman and Margaret Stephens
Art and editorial direction David Jefferis
Editorial revision Margaret Stephens
Text editor Eliot Humberstone
Design Iain Ashman
Design revision Robert Walster
Technical consultant Bob Currie
Illustrators Terry Hadler, Christine Howes, John Hutchinson, Frank Kennard, Michael Roffe, Robert Walster, John Scorey, Stephen Gardener, Chris Lyon and John Barker.

This edition published 1991.
Based on The Young Engineers Book of Superbikes, published 1978

Acknowledgements

We wish to thank the following individuals and organizations for their assistance.

Special thanks go to Tony Greener of Positive Images.
Matt Oxley
Auto-Cycle Union
Robert Cross
Dunlop Ltd
Griffin Helmets Ltd
Richard Powell
Glenn Wilson
Gerard Brown
Christopher Pick

Usborne Publishing Ltd
Usborne House
83-85 Saffron Hill
London EC1 8RT

Printed in Belgium

The name Usborne and the device ♛ are trademarks of Usborne Publishing Ltd.

Power

Maximum power on the first production bikes was a massive 110 hp. Kawasaki no longer state power outputs for their bikes, but we do know that today the GPZ900R's output is less, because of restrictions on noise and exhaust emissions. More important than power output is the spread of power available, which is excellent in this bike due to the use of four valves with each cylinder.

Naturally, big horsepower and top performance like this must be paid for and you cannot expect the fuel consumption of a moped. About 14 km per litre (39 mpg) is average, and gentler use of the throttle will give a maximum of about 19 km per litre (54 mpg).

The engine

This was the first Kawasaki engine to use four valves with each cylinder. Note the camchain is mounted outside the cylinder block. This means it is more accessible for service and cuts the engine width to 451 mm (18 in). Another feature helping to reduce the width of the engine is the position of the bores. The liquid cooling has allowed them to be placed close together. The balance shaft is mounted below the crankshaft.

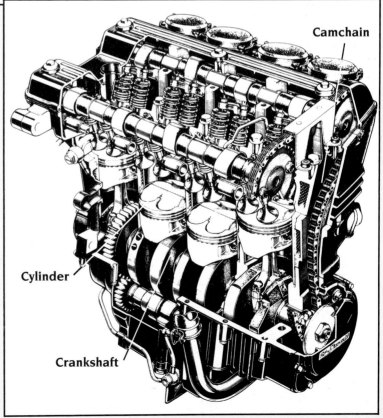

Camchain

Cylinder

Crankshaft

Ten international motorbike magazines voted the GPZ900R "Superbike of the Year" in 1984.

The first motorbikes

The first motorbikes ever invented were powered by steam and had three wheels. Then in 1869, Ernest Michaux from France developed a two-wheeled version, but it still had a steam engine. Michaux's motorbike was not a success. The engine was slow to start and not very powerful. The solid tyres made journeys very bumpy and worst of all, the engine's red hot boiler was far too close to the rider. Steam must have been a problem too, so the motorbike gave a very hot, sticky ride.

A far more practical model was developed in 1877 by the German engineer Nicolaus Otto. This motorbike had a petrol-driven internal combustion engine.

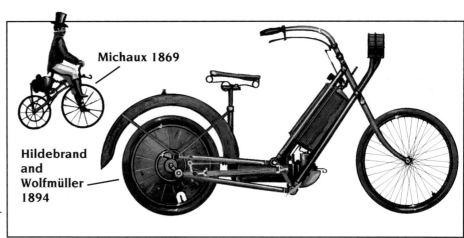

Michaux 1869

Hildebrand and Wolfmüller 1894

To the left is Michaux's steam motorbike. On the right is the world's first commercially made motorbike, the Hildebrand and Wolfmüller. This had a huge twin cylinder engine of 1,488 cc, which still holds the record for the largest engine on a production bike. The rear mudguard held water to cool the engine. There was a single brake, but the rider also used his foot to operate a steel lever which scraped against the ground. Top speed was 45 km/h (28 mph).

The first motorbike designers experimented with many different positions for the engine. The two designs here show the engine in rather bizarre positions. The most commonplace was above the wheels.

This is a 1901 Werner 262 cc. It was the first production bike with an engine placed between the wheels. Other manufacturers were quick to copy this design and modern bikes still have the same basic layout.

In 1901, this bike was built by George Hendee in the USA and called an Indian. Hendee only built three in 1901, but in the next two years produced a total of 568. The Indian was a classic American bike.

By 1907, motorbike speeds had passed the 200 km/h (124 mph) mark. Glenn Curtiss, an American who owned an airplane company, rode this machine on a beach in Florida, USA, at nearly 220 km/h (137 mph). Many people refused to believe that the bike was capable of such a speed, so the "record" was never made official. Curtiss had designed the engine for one of his airplanes, and fixed it to a motorbike frame to test it. The bike was never intended as a road-going machine.

Riding on air

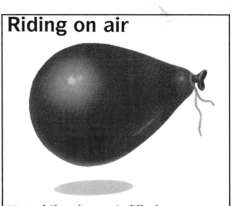

Motorbikes have air-filled pneumatic tyres which absorb bumps to give the rider a smooth ride. Blow up a balloon, fasten it securely and then gently sit on it. The cushion effect works in the same way as a tyre.

Since the early days of motorcycling more than 2,000 different makes of bike have been produced.

Motorbikes at war

Motorbikes have been useful during wars. In World War I, dispatch riders carried messages into battle zones where radio and telephone communications were few or non-existent.

Motorbikes even went into battle themselves, with machine guns mounted on sidecars. The picture below shows a BMW R75, first built in 1940. Over 16,500 R75s were used during World War II, and spearheaded blitzkrieg ("lightning war") attacks. They had a top speed of 95 km/h (59 mph). The Russian Army still uses a similar design today, called the K-M72. The diagrams below show the back, side and front view of the R75.

James and Royal Enfield both made lightweight 125 cc machines that could be dropped by parachute.

Classic bikes

From the early days of motorbikes until modern times, there have been some special machines that became famous for smooth performance, speed or other unique design features. These bikes are called "classics".

None of the bikes shown here is in production any more, but they will always be remembered as classic bikes of their time.

Choosing a selection of famous bikes is difficult as everyone has their own favourites. Make your own list and see how far you agree with the ones here.

Triumph Vertical Twin 650 cc. Top speed 135 km/h (84 mph), 1933-1983. This side-by-side engine was copied by many other manufacturers. One famous copy, the Triumph Bonneville had a top speed of 192 km/h (119 mph).

Harley-Davidson WLA 45, 738 cc, V-twin. Top speed 120 km/h (74.6 mph), 1937-1952. This powerful and reliable bike became well-known in World War II when 90,000 were issued to US and British troops.

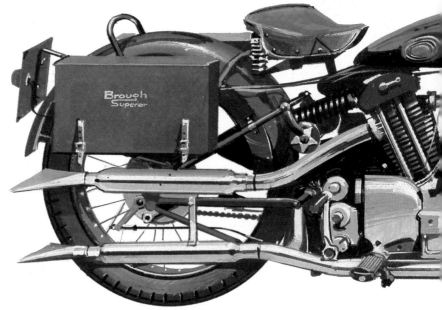

Ariel Square Four 500, 600, 1,000 cc models. Top speed 161 km/h (100 mph), 1929-1958. The "Squariel" engine was basically two parallel twins with their crankshafts geared together. This design gave excellent balance.

Vincent Black Shadow 998 cc V-twin. Top speed 197 km/h (122 mph), 1948-1955. This was the fastest production bike of the 1950s. It was famous for the superb quality of its craftsmanship and smooth performance.

Motorbikes have been made all over the world since the 1890s. But in the 1990s, Japan dominates the market.

Brough Superior

Brough Superior SS 100, 980 cc V-twin. Top speed 161 km/h (100 mph), 1924-1939. This was a luxury bike built mostly by hand and renowned for its smooth performance and craftsmanship.

Manx Norton 490 and 348 cc single cylinder. Top speed 195 km/h (121 mph), 1932-1962. The frame was known as a "featherbed" because it allowed great comfort at high speeds. A rigid steering head meant it handled well on corners.

Honda CB 750, 736 cc with four transverse cylinders. Top speed 197 km/h (122 mph), 1969-1986. This was the first of the modern Japanese motorbikes, it had an electric starter, a high cruising speed and excellent acceleration of 0-100 km/h (0-62 mph) in under 6 seconds.

Laverda Jota 981 cc transverse three. Top speed 227 km/h (141 mph), 1975-1982. This was an extremely fast road bike, well-known for its excellent handling at high speeds. It was originally developed by Laverda's British importers and was hand-built in Italy.

BMW R69S, 594 cc horizontally opposed twin engine. Top speed 161 km/h (100 mph), 1960-1969. This was a classic touring bike because it gave a fast comfortable ride with its rubber mounted engine, a vibration damper on the crankshaft and great suspension.

The first chromium plated metal parts of a motorbike appeared on a Rudge speedway machine in 1929.

Piston power

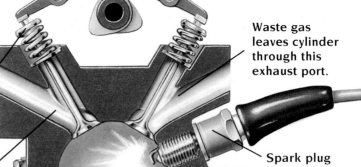

Four-stroke engine

There are two sorts of motorbike engine - two-stroke and four-stroke. Both types are explained on this page. Engines have one or more pistons, which move up and down inside the cylinder. They are powered by a gassy mixture of petrol and air. In a four-stroke engine, this mixture enters the top of the cylinder and there it is exploded by a spark from the spark plug.

The explosion forces the piston down, and this action then pushes down a connecting rod which turns the crank. A crankshaft runs through the centre of the crank and this turns too. The crankshaft transmits its circular motion to the back wheel by a chain or driveshaft.

The cam and valve system opens and shuts the ports in the correct sequence.

A mixture of petrol and air enters the cylinder through this inlet port.

Piston rings make the piston a gas-tight fit in the cylinder. Oil is used as lubricating fluid.

Most modern bikes have four-stroke engines which are more robust and emit less pollution than two-strokes.

The crank rotates moved by the connecting rod. The crank's rotating speed is measured in rpm - revolutions per minute.

Waste gas leaves cylinder through this exhaust port.

Spark plug

The cylinder's volume is measured in cc - cubic centimetres.

Piston

Cylinder

Connecting rod

Crankcase

Crankshaft runs through centre of crank.

The two-stroke engine

In a two-stroke engine the piston moves up and down twice between each spark. The petrol-air gas enters the crankcase below the piston. The piston moves down and pushes the gas up through an opening to the top of the cylinder. When the piston rises again it compresses the gas and a spark creates an explosion which pushes the piston back down, rotating the crank.

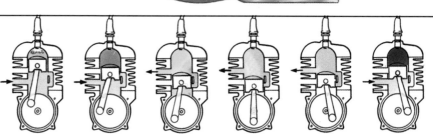

1 POWER - spark plug ignites gas mixture. Fresh gas in, waste gas out.

2 COMPRESSION - gas by the piston.

The four-stroke engine

The four-stroke engine moves up and down four times between each spark.
1. "Induction" stroke: gas is drawn through the inlet port into the top of the cylinder.
2. "Compression" stroke: the piston rises squashing the petrol-air gas. 3. "Power" stroke: a spark explodes the gas, pushing the piston down. 4. "Exhaust" stroke: waste gas is pushed out of the exhaust port.

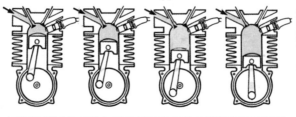

1 INDUCTION - gas mixture is drawn into the cylinder.

2 COMPRESSION - gas piston.

When an engine is working at 7,000 rpm, each piston goes up and down over 116 times every second.

Arranging the cylinders

Motorbike engines vary in the number of cylinders. Generally, the more cylinders they have, the smaller the engine vibration and the smoother the ride. Shown below are many different designs.

Flat twin   BMW R100S ▶

◀ Parallel twin
Triumph Bonneville

Transverse triple
Suzuki GT 750 ▶

◀ V-twin   Moto Guzzi 850

Flat-four
Honda Gold Wing ▶

◀ Transverse four
Kawasaki 650

Transverse six
Benelli Sei ▶

◀ Square four
Suzuki RG 500

Keeping parts apart

The magnified view on the right shows where the sides of the piston and cylinder come together. It is absolutely vital that they never actually touch each other. If this happened, the friction created would quickly destroy their surfaces.
  Keeping them apart is oil, which acts as a lubricant. This experiment shows how a lubricant can reduce friction.

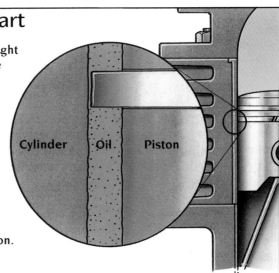

Cylinder   Oil.   Piston

Experiment

You need a small plastic cup and a tray. These will represent the cylinder and piston surfaces.
  Try skating the cup across the dry tray surface. Now place two large spoonfuls of water on the tray.

Small plastic cup

Skate the cup across the puddle. You will see that it goes much further and much faster than before because the water has acted as a lubricant and reduced friction between the surfaces.

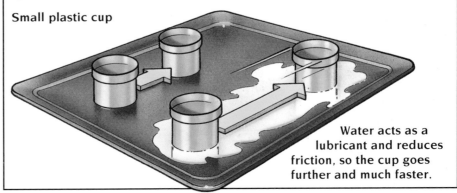

Water acts as a lubricant and reduces friction, so the cup goes further and much faster.

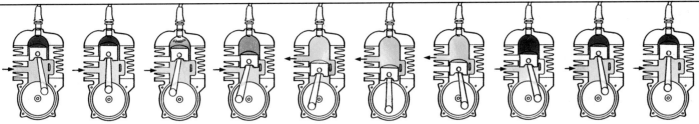

mixture is squashed
Fresh gas in.

1 POWER - spark plug ignites gas mixture. Fresh gas in, waste gas out.

2 COMPRESSION - gas mixture is squashed by piston. Fresh gas in.

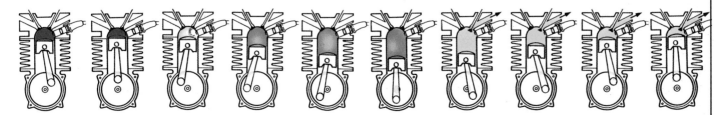

is squashed by the

3 POWER - spark plug ignites gas mixture. Explosion forces piston down.

4 EXHAUST - piston moves up pushing waste gas out.

In 1856 Moto Guzzi made a racing engine with 8 cylinders - the most ever.

Tyres and brakes

Tyres and brakes are the two most important pieces of equipment on a motorbike. If either become faulty then the life of a motorcyclist can be seriously endangered.

The front and rear tyres on a bike are of a different size and tread pattern as they have different jobs to do. The smaller front tyre is designed to resist slipping sideways on corners. It is also designed to pump water away from the rear tyre's path on a wet road. The bigger rear tyre is harder wearing and transmits the power of the engine onto the road. Most modern bikes have hydraulically operated disc brakes on both wheels.

The rear brake is operated by a pedal under the rider's right foot. On a good road surface 70% braking pressure should be applied to the front brake and 30% pressure to the rear brake.

A tyre's "rubber" part is often a mixture of natural rubber and butyl plastic. The tread is mostly butyl, but the side walls have up to 60% natural rubber.

Under-inflated tyres overheat at high speeds which shortens their life. Over-inflated tyres have a smaller area in contact with the road, causing instability.

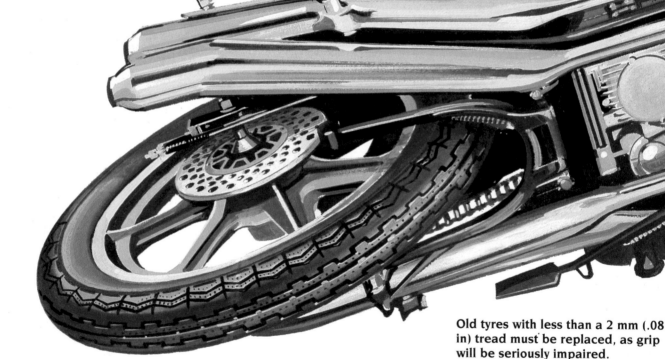

Old tyres with less than a 2 mm (.08 in) tread must be replaced, as grip will be seriously impaired.

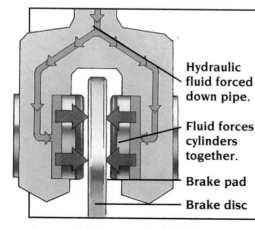

Hydraulic fluid forced down pipe.

Fluid forces cylinders together.

Brake pad

Brake disc

Disc brake stopping power

Hydraulic discs are fitted to motorbike wheels. When a rider operates the brake lever and brake pedal, the brake fluid is put under increased pressure. This fluid then presses on the brake pistons, forcing them along cylinders. The pistons are backed with brake pads. These push against the disc, creating friction and slowing the wheel down. With hydraulic brakes, it is important to keep the brake fluid topped up. Watch out for leaks and check regularly for wear and tear, replacing all worn parts.

Take a large coin and roll it on a smooth surface. Catch it between your finger and thumb. This is how two brake pads stop a moving wheel.

Rear tyres on racing bikes get very hot - up to 125°C when accelerating around banked bends

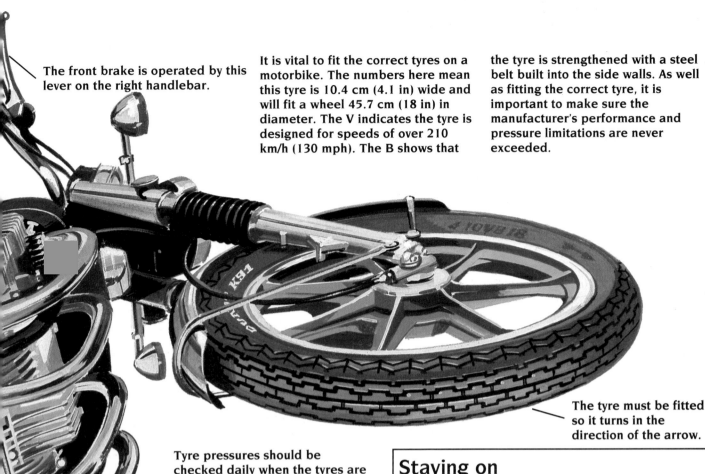

The front brake is operated by this lever on the right handlebar.

It is vital to fit the correct tyres on a motorbike. The numbers here mean this tyre is 10.4 cm (4.1 in) wide and will fit a wheel 45.7 cm (18 in) in diameter. The V indicates the tyre is designed for speeds of over 210 km/h (130 mph). The B shows that the tyre is strengthened with a steel belt built into the side walls. As well as fitting the correct tyre, it is important to make sure the manufacturer's performance and pressure limitations are never exceeded.

The tyre must be fitted so it turns in the direction of the arrow.

Tyre pressures should be checked daily when the tyres are cold. The treads should be inspected daily too for objects like stones and nails.

In 1888, John Dunlop invented the first inflatable tyre when he joined a length of hosepipe and fixed it around the wooden rim of a bicycle.

Types of tyre

To the right is the profile of a standard tyre. The tread pattern is designed to drain water away and grip the road. The tread goes up around the sides so the tyre can still grip when leaning into corners.

To the left is a "racing slick" which has a smooth surface. It is also "low profile", having a reduced depth compared to ordinary tyres. Both features mean more tyre comes into contact with the track giving big, powerful racing bikes extra stability.

Staying on

When moving in a straight line, gravity pulls the bike down and it is perfectly balanced. When turning into a bend, an outward force pulls at the bike and rider. It is important the rider leans the bike into the bend and aligns

his centre of gravity with the bike's. The weight of the bike and rider will then counteract the outward force.

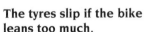

The tyres slip if the bike leans too much.

The bike and rider will tip over when the rider does not lean enough.

Protecting the head

In a motorbike accident, the head is the most vulnerable part of the rider's body. A human head weighs about 4.5 kg (10 lb). But if it hits something at 48 km/h (30 mph), the impact weight becomes 136 kg (300 lb) - rather like being hit with a massive hammer. It is vital that motorbike riders and passengers wear helmets.

Nowadays there are two types of crash helmet. The open-face helmet, like the 1950s design below, is less claustrophobic and usually cheaper. However, the full-face helmet, like the picture to the right, gives greater all-round protection.

Evolution of the crash helmet

Since motorbikes were first invented, the design of crash helmets has changed enormously. The pictures below show three of the major designs in motorbike history.

The pudding basin was made originally from leather. This design was first used in the 1900s.

This jet style open-face helmet was first used in the 1950s and is still worn today.

This is a modern full-face BMW System helmet which complies with the world's toughest safety standards.

Anatomy of a full-face helmet

This picture gives you an idea of the careful design that goes into the making of a modern full-face crash helmet. Safety standards for new designs are very tough, and all helmets undergo rigorous tests before they can be sold to the public.

A piece of grit hitting your eye at 40 km/h (25 mph) could blind you. This is why visors are essential. Scratches can give a distorted, dazzling effect at night. So all visors should have an anti-scratch coating. A few drops of washing-up liquid rubbed gently onto the inner surface will help prevent misting.

Never buy a second-hand helmet. Always spend as much as you can on a modern design. Fit is very important. Choose a helmet and then try it on before buying. Does it fit comfortably? When securely fastened does it move much, either backwards and forwards or side to side? If the answer is yes, then it is too big.

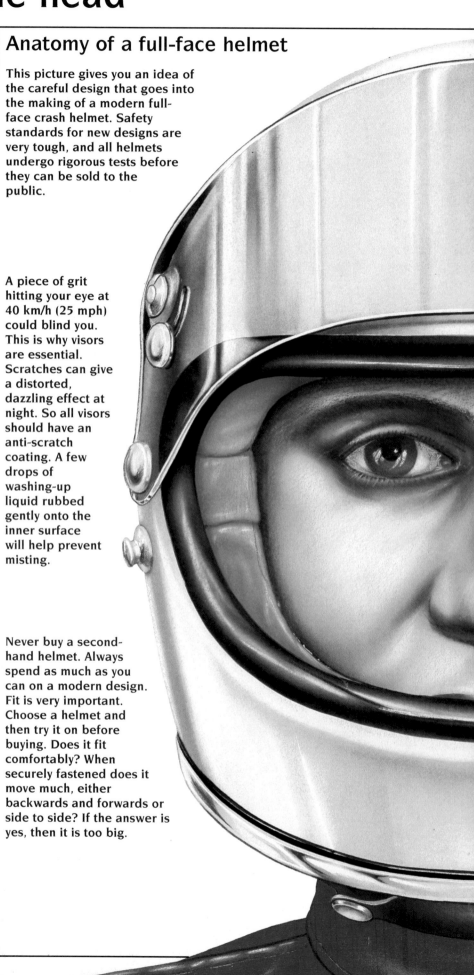

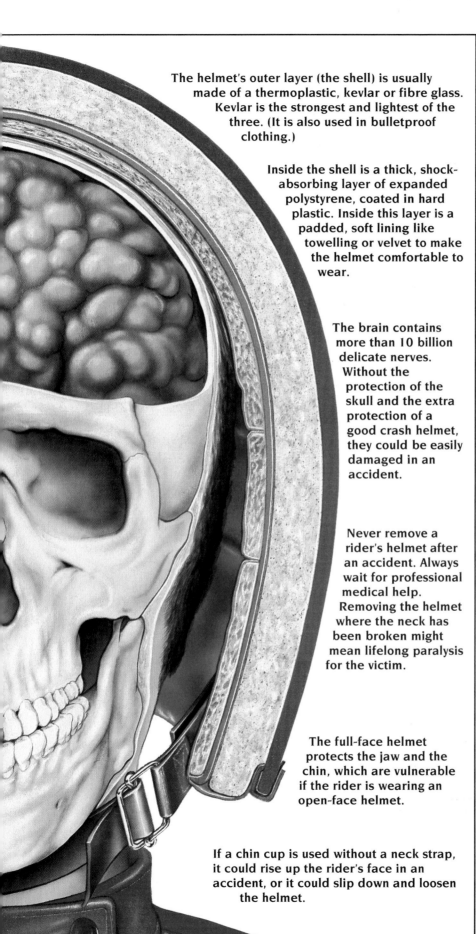

The helmet's outer layer (the shell) is usually made of a thermoplastic, kevlar or fibre glass. Kevlar is the strongest and lightest of the three. (It is also used in bulletproof clothing.)

Inside the shell is a thick, shock-absorbing layer of expanded polystyrene, coated in hard plastic. Inside this layer is a padded, soft lining like towelling or velvet to make the helmet comfortable to wear.

The brain contains more than 10 billion delicate nerves. Without the protection of the skull and the extra protection of a good crash helmet, they could be easily damaged in an accident.

Never remove a rider's helmet after an accident. Always wait for professional medical help. Removing the helmet where the neck has been broken might mean lifelong paralysis for the victim.

The full-face helmet protects the jaw and the chin, which are vulnerable if the rider is wearing an open-face helmet.

If a chin cup is used without a neck strap, it could rise up the rider's face in an accident, or it could slip down and loosen the helmet.

Easy riding

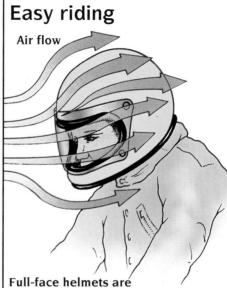

Air flow

Full-face helmets are aerodynamically designed to give less resistance to air at high speeds. This means air flows past smoothly at high speeds, which reduces noise and buffeting.

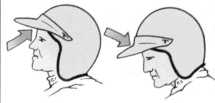

With an open-face helmet, air-flow at high speeds can catch under the peak (left), jerking up the helmet and head, which can be dangerous. If the driver has his head down, air can press down on the peak, straining the forehead and neck muscles (right).

A vision problem

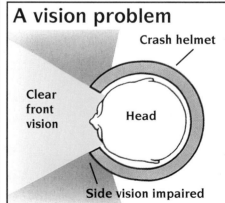

Crash helmet

Clear front vision

Head

Side vision impaired

The first full-face helmets only had small eye slits which impaired side vision. Later designs developed wider openings, but side vision is still not as good as with open-face helmets.

Motocross and trail bikes

These bikes are designed for rough conditions and must have excellent suspension and powerful engines to cope with the lumps and bumps of cross-country riding. Motocross bikes are special off-road racers ridden in club competitions. Motocross is an exciting sport with ditches that riders jump, steep downhill turns and usually a water splash at the bottom of a gully that turns into thick mud. Similar to motocross bikes, trials bikes are raced in cross-country trials events. But riders are timed instead of racing against each other as in motocross. Enduros are similar to trials but run over hundreds and sometimes thousands of kilometres or miles of country tracks and public roads. Trail bikes are modelled on motocross bikes but can be used on or off the road. These machines can perform as well over rough land as in busy city streets.

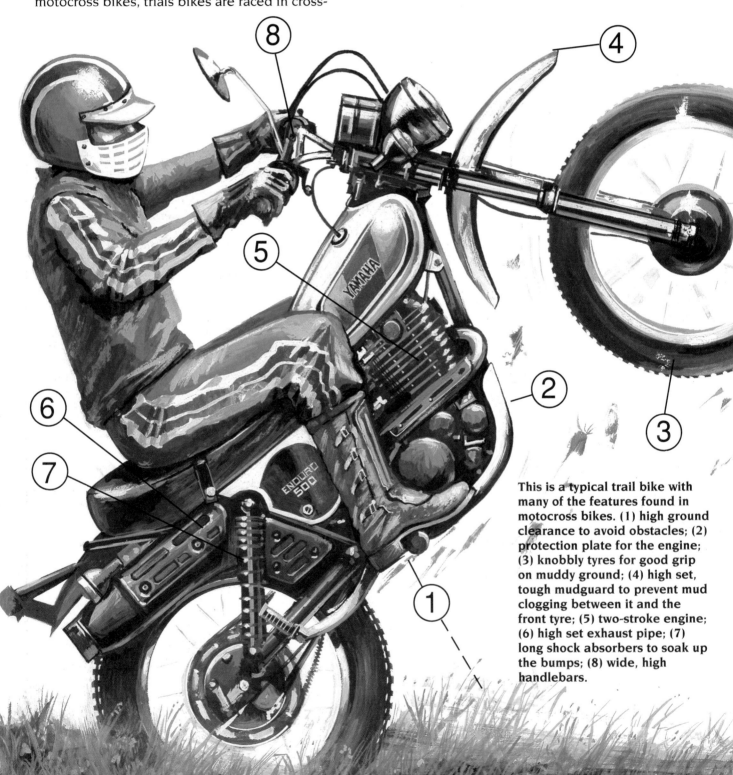

This is a typical trail bike with many of the features found in motocross bikes. (1) high ground clearance to avoid obstacles; (2) protection plate for the engine; (3) knobbly tyres for good grip on muddy ground; (4) high set, tough mudguard to prevent mud clogging between it and the front tyre; (5) two-stroke engine; (6) high set exhaust pipe; (7) long shock absorbers to soak up the bumps; (8) wide, high handlebars.

Absorbing the bumps

Shock absorbers have two main parts - a steel spring to absorb bumps and a piston connected to it. The piston slides up and down in an oil-filled cylinder. Its job is to slow down the bouncy movements of the spring. The diagram below shows an inside view of a rear shock absorber.

Oil or gas in cylinder.

Piston moves up and down with spring. Oil in the cylinder slows it down. This in turn damps the bounciness of the spring.

Spring compresses to absorb the shock of hitting a bump in the ground.

A modern trail bike

Suzuki DR 800

The Suzuki DR 800, otherwise known as Dr Big, has the world's biggest and most powerful single cylinder, four valve engine. With an engine capacity of 779 cc, the thumping power unit gives excellent turning power (torque) and top speed. Dr Big, like all trail bikes, is an off and on the road machine.

With dual spark plugs and an electronic self-starting system, the engine springs to life with first time reliability.

The superb suspension, the low centre of gravity, extra-slim frame and light weight make the bike easy to handle and very nimble over rough countryside. The centre of gravity is kept low by the position of the 29 litre (6.4 gallon) fuel tank.

One of the problems with trail bikes is the noisy engine, but Dr Big has an exhaust system which is fitted with twin mufflers to reduce noise levels.

The bike is designed in a snazzy colour scheme, and the comfortable seat is built for a passenger and rider, and specially designed for long rides. The seat has a luggage carrier and a grab rail for the passenger.

Other points of interest are hand protectors on the handlebars, a sump guard to protect the engine and gearbox from loose stones and a powerful halogen headlight.

Home-made shock absorber

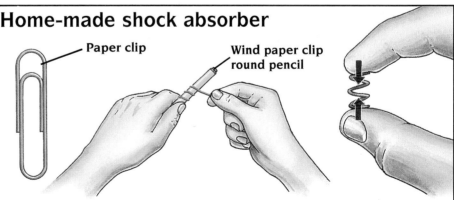

Paper clip

Wind paper clip round pencil

A shock absorber spring is one long piece of steel wound up to form a coil. The longer the coil, the more it can compress when the wheel hits a bump. The amount a coil can compress is called "travel".

Make your own mini shock absorber by straightening out an ordinary paper clip. Then wind it around a pencil, like in the picture above. When you take it off, you should have a small, springy coil.

Drag bikes

Drag bikes are the ultimate in racing machines. They are fast and furious, often with more than one engine, and race down a track that is only 402 m (¼ mile) long.

Riders compete against the clock in solo races, or against each other in pairs. Drag racing started in Britain during the 1920s, but it is now popular the world over, especially in the USA.

As the rider here revs up his machine at the start, fuel has been poured onto the track and set on fire to soften the tyres. This will improve their grip.

This bike is the "Atcheson Topeka and Santa Fe", ridden by Russ Collins. Russ held the 402 m (¼ mile) record in the 1970s with a time of 7.86 seconds.

This machine had no less than three engines. The 12 cylinders and 3,000 cc of power accelerated the bike to nearly 300 km/h (186 mph) in about 8 seconds. Competition solo drag bikes use fuels like methanol and nitro-methanol.

Drag racer controls are similar to an ordinary bike. But to cope with the enormous power, a heavy-duty clutch is fitted.

Countdown to a quick getaway

The riders are revving up and watching the "Christmas tree". This is a series of lights, one for each rider, which counts them down to the start signal. Light 1: approach the start. Light 2: bikes almost at the line. Light 3: bikes ready to race. Light 4: false start. Lights 5, 6, 7: ready, steady, go! Light 8: false start. As the bikes blast off they cross a light beam (A) starting an electronic clock. 402 m (¼ mile) later they cross the finish light beam (B). The clock then records the time. Light beam (C) is 1 m (3 ft 3 in) after the finishing line. The clock records the bikes from B to C to calculate their speed.

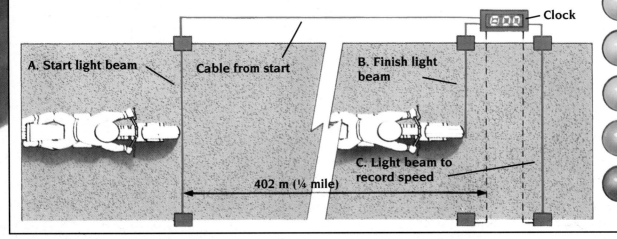

A. Start light beam

Cable from start

B. Finish light beam

Clock

C. Light beam to record speed

402 m (¼ mile)

1
2
3
4
5
6
7
8

The "Timetraveller" drag bike went from a standing start to 97 km/h (60 mph) in two seconds.

Speedway

Speedway is an exciting and popular sport staged in special stadiums all over Europe, Australia and the USA. Riders usually compete in teams and leagues rather like soccer. Races are run in quick succession, about one every five minutes, anti-clockwise around four laps of the track. The winning team is the one scoring most points.

Most speedway bikes are single cylinder, four-strokes with a clutch and twist-grip throttle. If race leaders braked quickly, nasty pile-ups could result. So the bikes have no brakes.

The speedway rider

The best riders in a team are called "heat leaders". The next best are "second strings" and the remainder are called "reserves". The fuel is pure methanol.

A speedway rider balances his bike by applying great power to the back wheel and opposite lock to the front wheel.

Riders rev up their engines behind a starting tape which only lifts when the referee judges everyone to be ready. Riders always hug the track's inside line and ride at a furious rate, sliding through corners with their front wheels turned sideways.

Speedway bikes have no gears.

Front suspension is minimal compared to other bikes .

Speedway racing is exhilarating and very dangerous. Riders must have excellent balance to judge bends accurately. Like many other sportsmen, they need to be good tacticians too, reading the race correctly and predicting what other competitors might do. Speedway is tough physically, and good all-round physical fitness, perfect eyesight and perfect hearing are musts.

Most important of all though is lengthy experience on a speedway bike. The bikes are so unlike other

machines, as they are light but very powerful, and no rider can get used to controlling a bike without brakes in a short space of time.

Speedway riders must have all-in-one leather riding suits, strong crash helmets and special boots. The left boot has a steel sole for sliding through corners. Another expensive necessity, apart from the bike itself, is a vehicle to transport the bike to races.

During the time it takes you to read this sentence a drag bike can accelerate from 0-300 km/h (186 mph)

Grand Prix

Grand Prix road racing takes place all over the world. There are four different classes depending on the engine capacity of the bike - 80 cc, 125 cc, 250 cc and 500 cc. A fifth class is for 500 cc bikes with a sidecar.

The winner of each race is awarded 20 points; second place earns 17 points and then a sliding scale of points - 15, 13, 11, 10, 9, 8, 7, 6, 5, 4, 3, 2 and 1 - is awarded down to 15th place. Each year, every class has a world champion. This is the rider who scores most points, although only the points from his seven best races throughout the year count towards the championship.

This is the Honda NSR500, a 500 cc world championship winning bike. It has been developed over eight years. One of the newest features of the motorbike is an on-board computer which controls engine timing and the exhaust valve.

The NSR500 weighs less than 120 kg (265 lb). Ground clearance is 105 mm (4 in) and overall width is 600 mm (2 ft). Fuel tank capacity is 30 litres (6.6 gallons).

The Honda factory in Japan is always improving the aerodynamics of the NSR500. The bike's air resistance (the drag factor) has been greatly reduced over the eight years of its development. This has been achieved by streamlining the bike's overall shape.

The youngest world champion ever is Johnny Cecotto. He won the 1975 350 cc title when only 19.

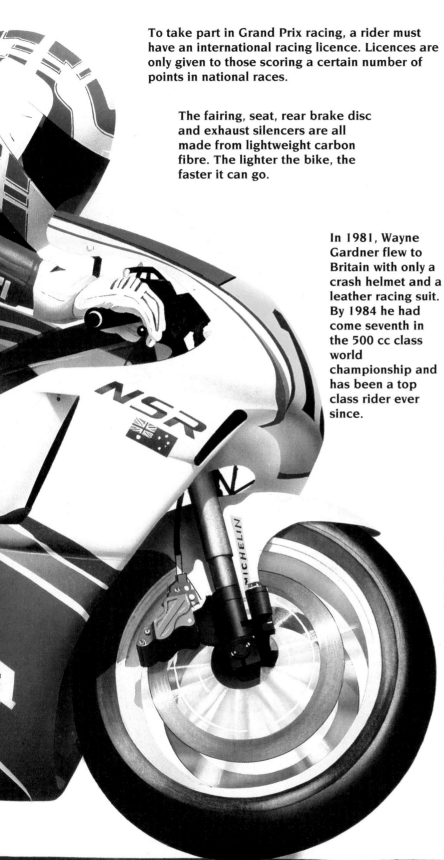

To take part in Grand Prix racing, a rider must have an international racing licence. Licences are only given to those scoring a certain number of points in national races.

The fairing, seat, rear brake disc and exhaust silencers are all made from lightweight carbon fibre. The lighter the bike, the faster it can go.

In 1981, Wayne Gardner flew to Britain with only a crash helmet and a leather racing suit. By 1984 he had come seventh in the 500 cc class world championship and has been a top class rider ever since.

Wayne Rainey ▲

Wayne Rainey from the USA won his first 500 cc world championship in 1990. Riding a Yamaha YZR500, he led the series from the first round and won seven Grands Prix in all. Out of the 44 Grands Prix he has raced so far, he has only failed to finish on three occasions which is a fantastic record for consistency.

Australian Wayne Gardner is shown racing the NSR500 here. Wayne won the 500 cc championship in 1987 on a version of the same bike and came second in 1988 to his great rival, the American Eddie Lawson, who was riding for Yamaha that year.

Grand Prix road racing is an expensive business. In 1984, when Honda were testing Wayne Gardner on the 500 cc Grand Prix circuit, he had to pay his own way. After coming seventh in the world championship that year, Honda gave him full financial backing. Most riders join a team like Honda, Yamaha Kawasaki or Suzuki.

Victory in the popular 500 cc class gives motorbike manufacturers valuable publicity for the bikes that they sell to the public. Companies like Shell or Michelin also get publicity by sponsoring the Grand Prix teams. In exchange for this advertising, the sponsors either pay or donate their product to the teams free of charge.

In 1989, Eddie Lawson joined Honda and began to ride the NSR500 with great success, winning the world title for the second year running.

Wheel sizes, front and rear, are 432 mm (17 in). Wheels are fitted with Michelin tyres.

The oldest world champion ever is Hermann-Peter Müller. He won the 250 cc title in 1955 at the age of 46.

Highway patrol

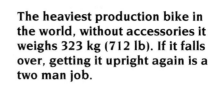

A modern city police force would be lost without a fleet of motorbikes. Weaving in and out of heavy traffic, motorbikes can speed medical assistance to road accidents and pursue escaping criminals down back roads or motorways. They also provide an escort service, like guarding cars carrying VIPs. Traffic control is another important duty and they deal with traffic jams and small traffic offences.

The heaviest production bike in the world, without accessories it weighs 323 kg (712 lb). If it falls over, getting it upright again is a two man job.

The fuel tank has a capacity of 22.73 litres (5 gallons). In the city, the bike runs at 13.6 km per litre (38 mpg).

American Harley-Davidson - Electra Glide

Harley-Davidsons are said to be the best bikes in the world for police work. They can keep up with most vehicles on the road and have a lot of sophisticated law enforcement equipment. The latest Electra Glide has a four stroke, air cooled, 1,340 cc V-twin engine. The seat is a "solo saddle" with air suspension for comfortable riding during long shifts.

At the rear, the Electra Glide can be fitted with a strobe light and an electronic 100 watt siren system. Officers communicate with their base by radio - a microphone is at the front of the bike.

Strobe light

Radio equipment

METROPOLITAN POLICE

A day in the life of a police motorcyclist

A typical duty for motorbike policemen is dealing with minor traffic offences. Here a motorbike rider has been stopped for going through a red light. The officer can act swiftly in heavy traffic.

Officers on bikes do not simply cruise about looking for trouble. They are assigned a "beat" and patrol a fairly small area. This one covers a major traffic junction and the approach roads leading to it.

A bank robbery has been committed and the criminals are about to flee the scene of the crime in a getaway car. Motorbikes will form a vital part of the police team in pursuing and stopping the runaways.

In May 1976, in Sydney, Australia, 14 policemen and 3 police women all rode on one bike - a 750 cc Honda.

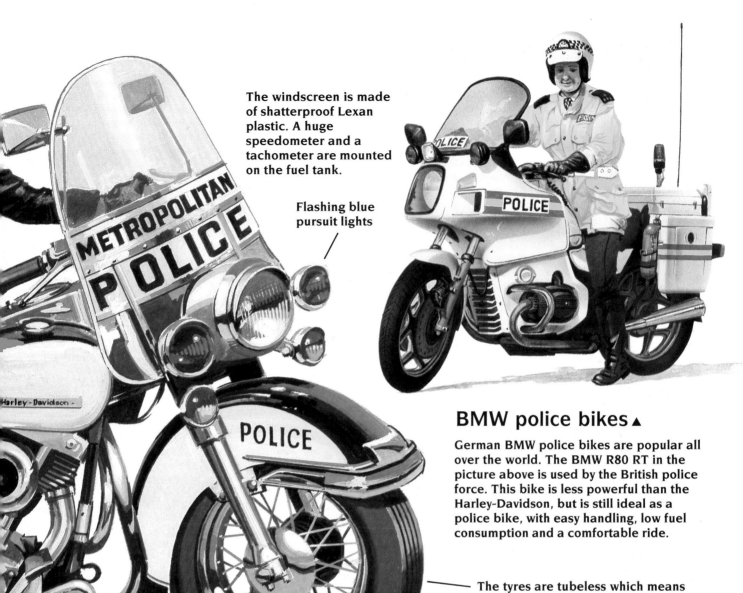

The windscreen is made of shatterproof Lexan plastic. A huge speedometer and a tachometer are mounted on the fuel tank.

Flashing blue pursuit lights

BMW police bikes ▲

German BMW police bikes are popular all over the world. The BMW R80 RT in the picture above is used by the British police force. This bike is less powerful than the Harley-Davidson, but is still ideal as a police bike, with easy handling, low fuel consumption and a comfortable ride.

The tyres are tubeless which means they are stronger and need less maintenance. Although Harley-Davidsons are expensive, they claim to consume less fuel and have lower maintenance costs than similar bikes.

The bank staff contact the police, giving details of the car. This information is radioed to all units near the bank, including officers on foot patrol, police cars and bikes, and sometimes even helicopters.

A patrolman hears the details on his VHF radio. He spots the car and calls HQ. His job is to trail the car and keep HQ informed. He will not intercept it as his bike could be damaged by the getaway car.

Guided by the patrolman, police cars move in and intercept the getaway car. In a dangerous situation like this, police cars are much better suited to stop and capture escaping criminals like these.

In the USA, one patrol cut its response time from 45 minutes in a squad car to 5 minutes on a Harley-Davidson.

Your first bike

When choosing your first bike decide how much you can afford and what you really want to use the bike for. Then pick a style that suits you best.

Remember, bikes with a small engine capacity cost less and have smaller running and maintenance costs. If you go for a sports roadster or trail bike, their good looks will cost more.

Always test the machine of your choice. Can you physically handle the bike? Can you walk it round in a circle with ease? Do you feel comfortable on it?

Suzuki AE50 Style. Two-stroke 49 cc engine. No gears. Seat height 610 mm (2 ft). Fuel tank capacity 4 litres (.9 gallon). This scooter is ideal for commuting around town, with no gear changes to worry about. Scooters like this are cheap to buy and run.
▼

Suzuki GP100. Two-stroke 98 cc engine. Five-speed gear box. Seat height 750 mm (2 ft 6 in). Fuel tank capacity 14 litres (3.1 gallons). An advantage with this bike is its large seat. A passenger can ride behind once you have passed your test.

◀**Kawasaki KDX 125SR. Two-stroke 124 cc engine. Six-speed gear box. Seat height 860 mm (2 ft 10 in). Fuel tank capacity 9 litres (2 gallons). This trail bike has the high, wide handlebars of a motocross machine.**

Yamaha TZR125. Two-stroke 124 cc ▶ **engine. Six-speed gear box. Seat height 765 mm (2 ft 6 in). Fuel tank capacity 12 litres (2.6 gallons). The frame is designed to give maximum strength with minimum weight, and was first used on Grand Prix racing bikes.**

◀ Honda NSR125. Two-stroke 124 cc engine. Six-speed gear box. Seat height 780 mm (2 ft 7 in). Fuel tank capacity 12 litres (2.6 gallons). Honda say that the bike's technology was developed on the Grand Prix racing circuit. The fairing makes it look very similar to a racing bike.

Kawasaki AR50. Two-stroke 49 cc engine. Five-speed gear box. Seat height 785 mm (2 ft 7 in). Fuel tank capacity 9.6 litres (2.1 gallons). This sportster has low handlebars for comfortable sports riding, good suspension for rough roads and lightweight cast alloy wheels. ▼

Remember!

Every country has different rules governing the type of bikes that young people can ride and how old they must be before being allowed on the road. It is essential that you check these details before buying your first bike.

There are other important details to sort out too. You will need a licence for yourself and tax and insurance for the bike. Remember, the bigger the engine capacity, the bigger your insurance costs.

Another important decision is how to pay for the bike. Cash is the best way, but if you need to borrow money then a bank loan or hire purchase may be necessary.

Learning to ride a motorbike

The most important lesson when learning to ride a motorbike is "safety first". This means wearing the correct clothing - a helmet, boots, eye protection, gloves and a tough weatherproof riding suit are essential.

Safe riding also means you must learn and obey all the rules of the road and take lessons from professional instructors. Frequent checks on engine oil, brakes, tyre pressures and back lights are also important.

Here are some of the things you must learn before riding on public roads. The bike in these photographs is a Suzuki TS 125R.

The first thing to learn is the layout of the controls. Motorbikes now have standard positions for the clutch, throttle, gear lever, front and rear brakes. Positions of minor controls like horn and light switches vary from maker to maker.

Most bikes have an electric starter, but you should learn how to kick start the engine into life, in case your starter motor fails or you have a flat battery. You can kick start either standing at the side of the bike, or astride it as shown here.

On a dry road apply 70% braking pressure to the front brake (above) and 30% to the rear brake. Never grab at the front brake lever. Use both brakes at once, but apply the front brake a fraction of a second before the rear brake.

It is easier to control a motorbike when going fast. On an instruction course you will be taught good bike control by riding slowly in a circle made from traffic cones. The clutch should be fully open and speed adjusted with the rear brake.

A slalom course develops your bike control skills even more. You will weave in and out of the cones as slowly as you can. Moving the cones even closer together tests how expert you are. You will need all these skills for slow road traffic.

Remember, as well as using your flashing indicator lights, you must still make hand signals when about to turn a corner. Always look behind before making a hand signal. Otherwise you might get your arm taken off by a car.

This is an emergency stop. The front suspension is compressed and the rear suspension is fully out. When making an emergency stop it is important to avoid applying the rear brake too fiercely as it may lock and then the tyre will skid.

! Do's and don'ts

● Wear a retro-reflective fluorescent overjacket if you can. This shines in the light of headlamps at night and glows brightly during the day.
● Buy the best helmet you can.
● Check that the bike is in neutral before starting the engine.
● Take extra care if the road is wet or the light is poor.
● Never overtake or change direction without checking the traffic behind.
● Never overtake on a bend or near the brow of a hill.

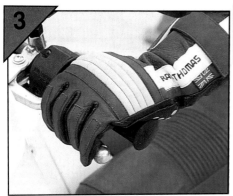

3

With the engine now running, move off by pulling in the clutch lever (picture 3) and pressing down the gear lever (picture 4) into first gear with your left foot. Then transfer this foot to the ground and bring up the right foot to cover the rear brake.

4

Open the throttle (picture 5) a little, gently releasing the clutch at the same time. As you start moving off, slow down the rate at which you are releasing the clutch and open up the throttle more. When you have pulled away you can release the clutch

5

completely. Co-ordinating the clutch and throttle can be difficult for beginners, so you will need to practise this. Before moving off always look behind and signal your intention to move out.

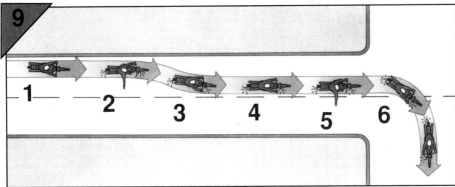

9

To turn a corner across oncoming traffic, first check the traffic behind (1) and signal that you want to cross to the centre of the road with your rear indicator (keep this on until you have turned the corner) and a hand signal (2). When it is safe, move to the centre of the road (3). Now slow down using the brakes and change gear as you approach the corner (4). Check behind you that it is still safe and give another hand signal (5). Turn the corner with both hands on the handlebars (6).

10

Almost all bikes have flashing indicator lights at the rear which signal which way you intend to go. Also at the rear are a brake warning light and a rear lamp for night-time riding. All lights, both rear and front, must be checked regularly.

T

The Suzuki TS 125R

This trail bike is light in weight and ideal for the learner rider. The 124 cc, water-cooled, two-stroke engine gives increased turning force (torque), and the front fork suspension is designed for bumpy off-road riding and the odd hole in the road. The chassis has good rear suspension.

The expansion chamber, fuel tank and radiator are positioned low down - all these features give the bike a low centre of gravity which is important for stability and handling.

The large, wedge-shaped knuckle guards help protect the rider's hands and a rear side grip is for pillion passengers to hold on to.

The world speed record

The world motorbike speed record is held by Californian Don Vesco. On 28 August 1978, Don and his bike Lightning Bolt managed a record of 512.7 km/h (318.6 mph).

Don Vesco has actually been the title holder since 1975 when he set a record of 487.5 km/h (302.9 mph) with the same bike, then called Silver Bird. Lightning Bolt was 6.32 m (20 ft 8 in) long and powered by two turbocharged Kawasaki Z1000 engines.

High-speed runs need a long track with a perfectly level surface. This was created for Lightning Bolt on the Bonneville Salt Flats in the USA, and stretched for 17 km (10.6 miles).

The 1975 version of this record-breaking bike, Silver Bird, had two Yamaha TZ750 two-stroke engines. Don Vesco tuned these engines to produce more power than their original capacity, and they ran on a mixture of petrol and oil.

A tail fin helped to keep the bike in a straight line and prevented instability during the high-speed runs.

The body was crafted from 1.5 mm (.06 in) thick aluminium. Lynn Yakel, the designer, later worked on Challenger, the US Space Shuttle.

To maintain good aerodynamic design, the exhaust pipe exited through a recessed hole at the top of the body.

The bike had two brake parachutes tucked into its rear end. These were essential after a high-speed run. One opened out to 3.7 m (12 ft) wide and ran out on an 11 m (36 ft) line. A larger 5.5m (18 ft) parachute was also carried.

The aluminium wheels were specially made for the bike and fitted with tubeless Goodyear tyres. The tyre on the rear driving wheel wore out after only two runs at top speed.

The body was mounted on a strong chrome-alloy frame.

Six steps in a motorbike speed record

Don Vesco eased his way into the cockpit for the 1978 world speed record attempt, while his crew made final adjustments. The two "skids" either side of the bike prevented it from toppling over at this stage.

A truck towed the bike along the track until it had gained enough speed to stay upright. At 80 km/h (50 mph) the tow cable was cast off and the truck then swiftly pulled clear of the track.

As the bike accelerated down the track, the "skids" retracted into the body. Don Vesco's right foot worked the throttle, while his left foot operated the clutch and his left hand changed gear.

Don Vesco lay in the bike. The distance between his body and the ground at the nose end was a mere 38 mm (1½ in).

The Flats are 1,310 m (4,298 ft) above sea level. So, engines were adjusted for low air pressure.

The best time to make a record-breaking attempt on the Flats is always in autumn after they have dried out over the summer.

A "skid" on each side kept the bike upright when at a standstill and at low speeds. The valve for the air pressure retraction system was in the left of the cockpit.

Safety at speed

This is the Kawasaki powered Lightning Bolt. Safety was a vital feature of the project and Don Vesco wore gloves, boots, a crash helmet and a fireproof suit. He was also strapped in with a five point seat belt and shoulder harness. The cockpit was lined with a 13 mm (½ in) thick shock absorbing material and there were two strong, anti-crush roll bars around the cockpit area. A freon-gas fire extinguisher was fitted with two outlets in the engine compartment and one in the cockpit. Electrical system isolating switches and fuel shut-off switches were installed to help avoid fire or an explosion in case of an accident.

The bike had to maintain its speed over a 1.6 km (1 mile) section in the middle of the track for the record to become official. Two runs were completed in each direction and the average became the world record.

At the end of the measured section the bike was slowed down by a high-speed parachute. If this parachute failed then an emergency chute was in reserve. The bike also had a single disc brake on the rear wheel.

After shattering the world record, the bike slowed down and the "skids" were lowered. Instruments on the bike showed approximate speed, but the electronic timing device on the track gave the official time.

Record Breakers

Between 1909 and 1978, the world motorbike speed record was broken 44 times. It was pushed up from 123 km/h (76.4 mph) to almost 513 km/h (319 mph).

Since then the world record holder Don Vesco has managed to achieve faster times, but never in both directions of the track, which is the rule for a world speed record.

The superior performance of engines and gear boxes and improved design giving better streamlining have made modern bikes much faster and safer. Many of these developments have come from lessons learned in racing and record breaking.

On these two pages you can read about some of the records, races and people who have earned their place in motorbike history.

Speed records

Early motorbike speed record attempts were made on race tracks and public roads.

As machines got faster, riders needed longer and straighter tracks. Greater length was needed because modern bikes take more time to develop maximum speed and it is only at maximum speed that a rider wants to cross the starting line of the timed section. Another reason for increasing the length of track was to give the fast bikes more slowing down distance.

Straight track is important, as going around bends slows bikes down and is highly dangerous at modern world-record breaking speeds. Most speed attempts are now run on the long, straight stretch of the Bonneville Salt Flats in Utah, USA.

In the chart on the right are some of the world speed records.

1909	W. E. Cook GB NL
1914	S. George
1920	E. Walk
1924	H. Le Vack
1930	
1935	
1937	
1951	
1955	
1962	
1970	
1975	
1978	
?	

The first track

Brooklands race track, situated near London, was the first racing circuit specially built for cars and motorbikes in the world. Brooklands opened in 1909 and was the centre of car and motorbike racing in England up until 1939, when the site was taken over for airplane production during World War 11. By 1939, the average lap record stood at 200 km/h (124.3 mph).

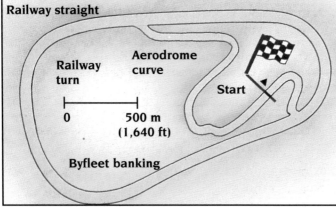

Railway straight

Railway turn

Aerodrome curve

Railway turn

Start

0   500 m
(1,640 ft)

Byfleet banking

The longest circuit

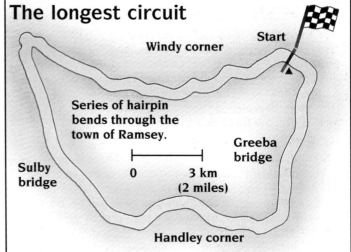

Windy corner

Start

Series of hairpin bends through the town of Ramsey.

Greeba bridge

Sulby bridge

0   3 km
(2 miles)

Handley corner

One of the most famous events in the racing calendar takes place in the Isle of Man, UK. Starting in 1907, the TT (Tourist Trophy) races were originally for ordinary bikes straight from the factory. The mountainous circuit of about 61 km (38 miles) covers twisting, hilly roads.

The fastest circuit

The Salzburgring in Austria is known as the fastest circuit in the world. It also has the reputation of being one of the most dangerous. Set in the mountains it is designed with many fast sweeping corners and has staged many exciting Grands Prix. Kevin Schwantz from the USA holds the record for the fastest lap. In 1990, he raced round the 4.24 km (2.63 mile) circuit at 195 km/h (121.2 mph), riding a Suzuki.

The fastest man for 14 years

99 km/h (76.43 mph)

151.43 km/h (94.10 mph)

dian 167.76 km/h (104.25 mph)

h Superior JAP   192.86 km/h (119.84 mph)

ht GB OEC-Temple JAP   244.20 km/h (151.75 mph)

E. Henne Germany BMW   257.74 km/h (160.16 mph)

E. Henne Germany BMW   281.35 km/h (174.83 mph)

W. Herz Germany NSU   291.76 km/h (181.30 mph)

R. Wright New Zealand Vincent HRD   299.70 km/h (186.23 mph)

W. Johnson USA Triumph   363.69 km/h (225.00 mph)

C. Rayborn USA Harley-Davidson   430.09 km/h (267.26 mph)

D. Vesco USA Yamaha 487.52 km/h (302.94 mph)

D. Vesco USA Kawasaki 512.73 km/h (318.61 mph)

?

Tailfin

Air inlet

Ernest Henne's 1937 world speed record of 281.35 km/h (174.83 mph) was set at Darmstadt in Germany on one of the first fully streamlined motorbikes. It is shown on the left. This was the last of the seven world records that Henne set in the 1920s and 30s. It lasted for 14 years.

The standing km

Don Vesco's world speed record is timed over a "flying" km (.6 mile), a measured section of track that the rider approaches very fast after a long run-up. A "standing" km (.6 mile) has no run-up and the rider is timed from the moment his bike starts to move, although he is allowed to rev up his engine. Drag bikes are used for this record.

Date	Rider	Machine	Speed
1967	Alf Hargon	JAP 1,149 cc	188.14 km/h (116.9 mph)
1972	Dave Lecoq	Volkswagon Dragwaye 1,286 cc	191.48 km/h (118.99 mph)
1975	Henk Vink	Kawasaki 1,081 cc	195.39 km/h (121.42 mph)
1977	Henk Vink	Kawasaki 984 cc	215.83 km/h (134.12 mph)
1986	Christian Le Liard	Honda Elf 1,000 cc	181.32 km/h* (112.67 mph)

* This is according to the new 1978 method of speed calculation.

500 cc world champions

Since 1949, motorbike Grands Prix have been organized by the FIM (Fédération Internationale Motorcycliste). There are different classes based on engine capacity and the fastest and most exciting class is 500 cc.
I = Italy; GB = Great Britain; R = Rhodesia; USA = United States; Aus = Australia.

Year	Rider	Machine	Nat	Year	Rider	Machine	Nat
1953	G. Duke	Gilera	GB	1972	G. Agostini	MV	I
1954	G. Duke	Gilera	GB	1973	P. Read	MV	GB
1955	G. Duke	Gilera	GB	1974	P. Read	MV	GB
1956	J. Surtees	MV	GB	1975	G. Agostini	MV	I
1957	L. Liberati	MV	I	1976	B. Sheene	Suzuki	GB
1958	J. Surtees	MV	GB	1977	B. Sheene	Suzuki	GB
1959	J. Surtees	MV	GB	1978	K. Roberts	Yamaha	USA
1960	J. Surtees	MV	GB	1979	K. Roberts	Yamaha	USA
1961	G. Hocking	MV	R	1980	K. Roberts	Yamaha	USA
1962	M. Hailwood	MV	GB	1981	M. Lucchinelli	Suzuki	I
1963	M. Hailwood	MV	GB	1982	F. Uncini	Suzuki	I
1964	M. Hailwood	MV	GB	1983	F. Spencer	Honda	USA
1965	M. Hailwood	MV	GB	1984	E. Lawson	Yamaha	USA
1966	G. Agostini	MV	I	1985	F. Spencer	Honda	USA
1967	G. Agostini	MV	I	1986	E. Lawson	Yamaha	USA
1968	G. Agostini	MV	I	1987	W. Gardner	Honda	Aus
1969	G. Agostini	MV	I	1988	E. Lawson	Yamaha	USA
1970	G. Agostini	MV	I	1989	E. Lawson	Honda	USA
1971	G. Agostini	MV	I	1990	W. Rainey	Yamaha	USA

Index

Going further

Bookshops and libraries are full of books about motorbikes and there are many magazines on the subject too. Here is a small selection of the publications available:

Books

Observers' Book of Motorcycles, Penguin
Custom Motorcycles, Andrew Morland, Osprey Publishing Ltd
First Bike, Kris Perkins, Osprey Publishing Ltd
Motorcycle Parade, Bob Holliday, David & Charles

Harley-Davidson - a celebration of the dream machine, Graham Scott, Hamlyn

Magazines

Classic Bike
Classic Motorcycle
What Bike
Motorcycle News
Classic Racer
Bike